Driver Side Window

Poems and Prose

Driver Side Window

Poems and Prose

CLAIRE MASSEY

Cover Design: Luke Wallin
Book Design: Diane Skelton

ISBN: 9798846316065

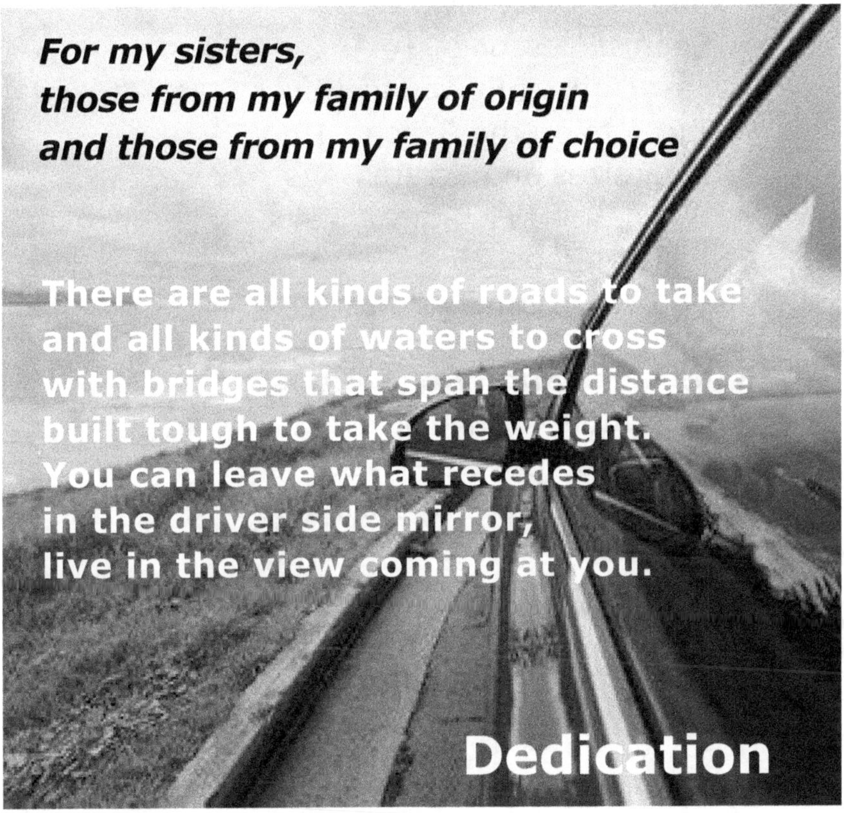

For my sisters,
those from my family of origin
and those from my family of choice

There are all kinds of roads to take
and all kinds of waters to cross
with bridges that span the distance
built tough to take the weight.
You can leave what recedes
in the driver side mirror,
live in the view coming at you.

Dedication

CONTENTS

PHOTO BY CLAIRE MASSEY

Island of Lost Boyfriends

IT HELPS TO compartmentalize. I like the word. Mentalize a compartment. Boyfriends of late teens, tender twenties, have been banished to an island in my head, an atoll of sand and coral rubble, arising from the jagged reefs, the dormant volcanoes that comprise the undersea of my neocortex. I've created an outcropping, like the archipelago where outcast eighteenth century Aussies were dumped, sentenced to isolation and hardscrabble living.

Not all the boyfriends are shanghaied. Not Bernie, master of verbal repartee, gleeful when I boomeranged barbs. Not Arthur, WWII aficionado, enthralled with a steady who interviewed WASP fly-girls at the vintage air show. He was proud when I earned accolades from the journalism club.

But Jack...strong-backed, marathon lover, vain of his Nordic nose, his mane of titian colored hair, he's a different story. Always tossing his head like an ungelded thoroughbred, eyes cavorting, averting his ears from my needy recitation of Mom's hospitalization or a pregnant cousin's impending ruination. Always trolling the length of our favorite bar, sonar pinging off any available blond. He's relocated to hindsight's epicenter.

Jeff too, a huge mistake, poster boy for steroid abuse, is consigned to my isle of the displaced. His

MO was ambush at Godfather's Pizza or Longhorn Steaks, his mantra, *Hey Ms. Liberated, you gotta job. I don't. Pay up.* When I summoned the nerve to ask why not ERA, he called me a *Femi-Nazi*. He examined my shapely legs, pert high-chested breasts, decided nice assets but not worth budding challenges to machohood.

Brad dwells on this geological uplift of mind, this topographical design of the thalamus. He rode Hondas while jonesing for Harleys, a short-fused guy out of patience with novices. Lacking the mettle to be a motorcycle mama, I leaned away from him in curves, leaned farther when he urged an Ectasy-fueled threesome. He kicked me to the curb at some country store, had to call my girlfriend for a lift home.

My island isn't lethal but time is relentlessly linear. These bad boys will age if not mature. I've left a cache of sunglasses so they won't burn their retinas and bottles of Coppertone, albeit expired and not high numbers. I've thrown in books by Gertrude Stein and Virginia Woolf, tales of survival from Zora Neale Hurston. Mother Nature is by turn indifferent, or in a mood to discipline disrespectful sons. She calls forth Amazon ants from the walls of driftwood shelters, floods them with rot, blows them apart. Feast or famine is Mother Luna's decision. Minuscule anchovies or egg-laden she-crabs. It's all in the crest of her tides, the whim of her phases.

Jack's back will ache and his head will bald. He'll stop seeking his reflection in after-storm puddles that crater quicksand. Jeff's muscles will elongate, unbunch, as he shimmies up palms and runs the perimeter for washed up sushi. Deprived of red meat and artificial testosterone, he'll crave coconut milk, contemplate fate like a fledgling monk. Brad has nothing to ride, no boat to drive beyond bone-crushing breakers. Still, he wants to get high, wonders if he should try a bite of lionfish or oleander.

Prodigious talkers, these smooth operators will one-up each other with conquest stories. They'll never figure I'm the common denominator, put a name to the ex with the endless legs and overblown imagination. I was one of a legion of girls on the serpentine route to womanhood, rehearsing smiles till it hurt, swallowing uncomfortable words, questioning if Eve really did ruin the world. We combed Cosmo for conversation starters, nodded when the quarterback denied there were female pilots. Heads cocked at inquisitive angles, we longed for dialogue, settled for monologue.

Should this trio appear in a dream I'll forget before waking, ask for second chances, a seismic shift in my thinking, I'll offer a test. *Convince me you remember.* Name the lost girlfriends who didn't know they could stand on their own, legs gangly yet resilient as a colt's. Name nine Greek muses, the feminine chakras, the seven sisters, Minerva's domains, "harvest moon" in eight languages, the maternal ancestors who gave you birth. Do this seventy times seven times and maybe, I'll revisit my seat of higher judgement, re-examine the molten heart of my own Vesuvius.

Outliers

Snorkeling past the divemaster's whistle,
Trinidad fades
to outline shaded
where jungle erupts,
no hint of interiors lush with scarlet ibis,
poinciana forest.

I float in the original womb
over gardens of staghorn coral blooming
with rainbow wrasse and fairy basslet,
intruder in a queendom ruled
by angelfish and barracuda.

The iguanas whose place it is
to recycle seeds of papaya,
the frigate birds who rule the air
above Mayaro, leafcutter ants
who work their metropolis unaware
of diners on verandahs overhead,
blind moles who tunnel under
golden shower trees
do not know this liquid warmth,
the buoyancy of salt.

Before me yawns a chasm shaded
cerulean-blue to black,
a launching slip atop a cliff
of continental shelf.

I move my hands in figure 8s,
quiet pumping legs.
Purple fans that guard the brink
wave me ahead
but I feel colder borders, understand,
I'm ill equipped to venture past them.

I turn back for the boat, the captain's count of souls,
the dry towel and box lunch.

Shore bound with all aboard,
the first mate tells us stories.
I take on faith his word
that bioluminescent creatures roam
sunless depths below
and ichthyologists discovered
opahs, warm-blooded fish,
flapping heated fins like wings,
swimming unmapped leagues beyond
the boundaries of their niche.

PHOTO BY LUKE WALLIN

Subtext of a Prayer

Wouldn't it be sublime
if Buddhists and Hindus,
Plato and Socrates,
had been right to tout
alternate designs
for atonement,
orders allowing
bonus seasons, lifetimes for amending
karmic grievances?

Who wants an eternity
of retrospection
in some white infinity
unmercifully distant
from this blue planet?

We pray for redemption
by whatever means
the master planner decreed
but what we want
is the easy penance
of Return, another April to flirt
with green-eyed spring, court
her tease of sun on skin,
brush of plumpened lips
and then,
her loamy breath, the quickening kiss.

Spanish Lessons

I think the Spanish lessons
are my little prayers
composed haltingly, earnestly
and offered up after work, twice a week
while the sun goes down.

The bankers that employ me
pay for the lessons,
candles purchased in an unholy church
of their own.
Still, I feel grateful. And guilty.
They want accounts.
I want to say,
How is it for you here?
Do you miss your sunny rivers,
your sea of Popsicle blue?

Cincuenta says the teacher. Fifty.
Sesenta. Sixty.
Setenta. Seventy.
Ochenta. Eighty. An entire span of life.

I am six months past fifty.
Tengo cincuenta anos.
Will I ever use this language
in a land that sanctifies it?

I want to stand beside a lake *(lago claro)*
in such a country, ask to rent
a small boat *(lancha pequena)*
from which to watch
the sun's descent.
?Para sesenta minutos o tres horas o todo dia?
I will take the all-day deal.
The proprietor smiles,
 !Que bien! He describes
the richness of the sky *(!los colores!)*
I will understand.

But after Spanish lessons...
will I speak only in prescribed exchanges,
perfunctory greetings,
while the joy of new words *(palabras nuevas)*
fades to weary repetition
of debits, deposits, terse *noticias* describing
restrictive time limits.

Will I spend my days
(even they are numbered)
telling and retelling
the unalterable times of *cambia dinero.*
Yes, we close at five. Twelve on Saturdays.
Si, cerramos a las cinco, el Sabado a doce.

Will I cease to learn, my phrases rote,
not prayers but a catechism
which produces
no exchange, no response.

Photo by Bart Daughety

Last Light at
Suwannee River State Park

A small, sacred place,
campsite number nineteen.
Trees use new sprung leaves
to knit a shawl
veiling engines and chatter
so that branches can whisper
liturgy
to one another.

Awakened by communion
above their sphere,
fireflies waft, drift,
illume low, shadowed bushes,
unaware they incarnate
light,
weave gilded thread
through the hem
of a nun's habit.

Tantrum on the Beach

THE GIRL CHILD is three. Baby fat knees flatline into stubby feet spread in combat stance, interred in wet sand. The mother looms above, forms a feature-less shadow that blocks the sun.

No, says the child. ***No.*** Cheeks contract. Face contorts. Eyes that were huge and all seeing shrivel, slit. Exposed thumbs grip balled fists. The mother has observed children who, at such moments, protect their thumbs, nest them under fingers, perhaps signaling they don't mean their tantrum, the outcome negotiable. Not her daughter.

The mother, comparative lit ex-grad assistant, is a scholar of lexicons, linguistics. She decides on verbal reasoning. "We've been here all morning. Dad's going to barbeque chicken this evening. You like chicken. You need to rest. Then, we'll make a salad. And red Jell-O." Her voice is chirpy, full of promise, as if she is hailing a new day instead of closing this one.

The child is having none of it. She has seen the silver wink of airborne mullet in the talons of the osprey. Her ears have detected the primal rhythm of ebb and flow. Transparent shallows magnified her toes. With a newly perfected pincer grasp, she filled a pail with coquinas. And still they offer themselves.

The child can speak sentences if she wants. But

she has moved through this morning in mute wonder. No word weights the buoyancy she has discovered. Her salt puckered lips, the egret overhead, the ghost crab with upraised claw are not metaphors; that is the province of the mother. This moment does not stand for any other. There is no reason, could never be a reason, to leave this place. Nothing better comes after. The child understands. It is the mother who is blinded, wrong-headed, misguided.

The battle ensues. The child wails in outrage, stiffens limbs, bunches muscles. Though sand sucks at the soles of her feet, reluctant to let go, mother too is a force of nature. She wields the power of a rogue wave. The child is lifted up and swept away.

Hours later in the rented summerhouse, the mother has put the child to bed in a coolly darkened room on a pillow soft mattress.

In an alcove off the kitchen with a west facing view, the mother watches three o'clock clouds dilute light. A disciple of verse, of nomenclature, she opens her journal, writes: *I marvel at the ferocity with which she fights naps. I'm afraid...*she crosses through afraid, writes *fear* (more poetic). *I fear that hers is a soul that will never...*(what is the apt word, submit? succumb?) *surrender to that good night. Those who will not go gently suffer.* She closes the journal with what she labels wistful sadness, regret on behalf of her daughter.

Behind the door of the guest bedroom, the child has discovered where to stand on the bed to push up blinds that shroud the east window. She dances and whirls, bounces on layers of foam, oblivious to a fading sun. At the height of her upward excursions, she sees sand and water merge in a communion of color she cannot yet name. Her heart beats faster.

Too late for any parent to save her, the child met, on the beach this morning, unutterable beauty. She was, as the mother knows (though the knowing defies rendering in words) utterly defenseless against such pull, so pitifully overpowered, already irredeemably, irretrievably in love.

Cigarettes and Scratch-offs

Cap turned backwards, he studies the line
a machine assigned with the permanent squint
of the Marlboro man who takes his chances,
eschews sunglasses. Between sullied thumbs,
sinewy arms lift the paper-thin
goldrush ticket like a consecrated wafer offered
to the glare hard sky of the auspiciously numbered
7-11, as if Ra might descend
from fluorescent heaven,
bless the luck of his draw, command Ramses
the builder to draft this gambler an empire.

He plunks eight dollars in quarters
on the counter for a double pack of Newports,
smiles sheepishly as the clerk laboriously
counts every one. Explains
he's fresh from the laundromat,
flush with change. Asks those of us waiting
our turn,
howyadoin'?

How *am* I doing? I wonder later
from the comfort of my delicately lighted sofa
as I down another glass of Bordeaux,
thrill to a PBS documentary
probing ancient Greek divination,
dream of a sojourn to the Delphi Oracle,
an odyssey I can afford.

Later still, I'm charmed
by the twist at the end of an O. Henry story,
prompted by the master of capricious fortune
to pick up my lucky pen,
stake it like a winning ticket
between manicured fingers,
fashion my own flash fiction
in which random numbers play no role
and Fate performs exactly as I envision.

Why Can't I Meditate?

Is it the slow clock ticking, signaling battery low,
like an aged heart losing
sinus rhythm? Is it the hurrying arc
of a northern sun, the furtive warbler
glimpsed this morning but not yet heard?

Perhaps it's the green light blinking
on the modem, something in my DNA,
hunter, gatherer, restless roamer.
Or the words for a poem
whirling like unruly kids
playing musical chairs in my head.

Why so hard to uncross arms,
rotate wrists to open palms?
Must be something in the posture
that offers the chest, exposes ribs,
unfists fingers to stretch and spread.
Why so awkward, so foreign an act,
to unfurl hands, relinquish the urge to grasp,
succumb to the lightness of air?

Night Heron

Patient as God,
divine in his sphere,
the night heron waits.

On the border of darkness,
in a sacred realm,
where land bows to water
and the downed sun yields
to the evening star,
he waits
for the cloud
to free the moon.

He lets
the fish decide
its fate.

In a Wayward Garden

WHILE CLICKING THROUGH infomercials on antenna TV, my husband of thirty-two years mentions that his ex-girlfriend never answered his last emailed *how's it going* inquiry. I say "Oh?" with a minimum of interrogative surprise so as not to rouse alarm.

Mariah has been drunk the better part of a decade. A few years ago, she smashed her hip, stumbling stupefied about the cabin she once shared with my husband. It's been oxycontin, unopened bills and bourbon ever since. "Maybe had to hock her laptop?" I venture.

"Hope it hasn't come to that. She's wheelchair bound, nothing to do *but* answer emails." Mariah was the girlfriend of my husband's freebird era, his misspent youth. She was muse of his halcyon days of writing protest songs, smoking weed, marching to end war and save whales. Hand in hand they passed beyond the doors of perception, quoting Kahlil Gibran and Jim Morrison.

"Doesn't mean something's happened," I say, though I'm sure that it has, as sure as I am of the mourning to come for their severed tether. Like the short end of a wishbone, the knowing snags in the soft tissue of my throat.

My husband mutes an actor ballyhooing spray-on make-up. He glances at the computer. "I'm going to google for an obituary."

He finds one, though it's terse, too sparse to mark anyone's passing. He calls Mariah's cousin to fill in the blanks. She might have overdosed, who knows, says the cousin. A neighbor from two hollows over came by to weed her garden, found the wheelchair overturned amid ragged columbine and Mariah resting comfortably on her side, if you can say that of the dead, fitted in the furrow between squash vines and sunflowers.

Mariah lived alone off the sole road on a mountain's backside, wouldn't sell the cabin my husband built for her. Told the doctors, the bankruptcy lawyers, even the cousin to get lost when they hyped the nursing home.

Our friends will tell you unequivocally: I rescued my husband from an aimless future as wandering minstrel. I saved him from acting the Tarot card fool with a flute, stepping off cliffs to fall in the abyss. I corralled a meandering spirit, rechanneled misdirected energy, convinced him to become a real builder, though he still won't work for track house developers or contract with clear cutters, never mind the boost it would mean for our IRAs. When we first got together, in the post-Mariah years, he doubted we should have children, still worried about greedy Homo sapiens overpopulating. I argued we had the right, the duty to reproduce. Our older son is in law school and the younger, thank God, changed his major to business writing. He was spinning poems I thought obtuse, sci-fi stories based on silly premises but we nudged him to study something more lucrative, marketing, advertising copy, the psychology of persuading others to consume. Like his father before him, our first-born veered into music, composing jazzy-blues hybrids that would never earn a living. Now he's on solid ground, writing scripts for commercials, no yawning chasms in *his* future.

I ask if there's to be a memorial service, a celebration of life. My husband shakes his head no, says, "I'm taking Danity out." I'm grateful because it's starting to rain. Our little Shih Tzu hates any form of humidity. She shakes and quakes and pulls me towards home at the skimpiest drizzle.

I've known better than to talk against Mariah. I've tolerated their (mostly) virtual friendship with grace and elan. It wasn't much of a hurtle, as she lived three states over and we've hardly encountered her, once at a gallery debuting her creepy paintings of wraith-like creatures (can't imagine paying for one) and later at the funeral of a mutual friend. Doesn't hurt that I have the patience of Job, the good judgement to bite my tongue when my husband reminisces about his peace and love years. The two of them worked part-time crap jobs for the sake of their *art*. They greeted mornings with green tea and tai chi, howled at blood moons from the mountaintop, scrounged gas money for whatever journey of enlightenment brightened their twin gypsy auras. Meals were earthy, colon friendly: beetroot, soy burgers, pumpkin muffins,

Photo by Luke Wallin

rhubarb pie, no beef or pork. As soon as we started dating, I set my husband straight on the need for real protein. Would you believe, he evolved into quite the grill master, his prime rib succulent, buttery tender.

Since Mariah died, my husband's forays down memory lane are growing frequent, strange and too public for comfort. After thirty-two years, love is not so physical but you're making love, aren't you, when you listen with rapt attention to rambling stories about the foundling dog he and his bell-bottomed Venus raised. Zeus had the phenotype of Disney's shaggy dog; the genotype of the outback's dingo. With the dingo's disdain for artificial safety, his loathing of man-made spaces. At dinner parties and art receptions, at book launches and barbeques, in the middle of our community pool, my husband venerates Zeus. *There was no way* he tells everyone within earshot—*even when icicles stiffened his belly fur and he clinked like cheap windchimes when he walked—that Zeus would enter the blanket lined doghouse with the cedar shake roof.* Uneasy guests glance my way, discomforted friends pour themselves another glass of merlot but I don't look away or ask the price of a barrel of oil or drift to the canapes table. I listen like a priest in the confessional, the indulgent mother of a toddler, a counselor of the bereaved, a cocked head terrier straining to understand human language. I listen with solid, steadfast presence, self-effacing generosity of spirit and that's the ungrudging essence of higher love, isn't it?

Sidetracks & Waystations

Photo by Luke wallin

A Formula for Entropy

NO ONE ELSE could do it. They're all gone now. So I stepped up to the proverbial, virtual plate of Book-ItQuick.com, half hoping there wouldn't be a seat. There was. Now I'm stuck, for a few days at least, breathing leftover air in Drunk Uncle's dilapidated little house in Bemidji, Minnesota. Yep, that's what we called him, lingo courtesy of an SNL sketch.

Drunk Uncle was the youngest of Dad's siblings, a scheme hatching, handout seeking, blame bestowing, ne'er-do-well. Except for Uncle, they all managed to escape the frozen tundra by the age of consent, fleeing a tyrannical father and a milquetoast mother, opting for life in warmer climes, where the blood flowed easy and sun warmed inhalations expanded minds as well as lungs. Like a sticky papered fly, Uncle's buzzing grew fainter over time, frozen as he was in place. Until a week ago, when his spirit, immobile as his body, catapulted to Someplace Else.

This chilly dawn, I've been tracking a kitchen stink to its epicenter. My flashlight illuminates a half-eaten can of tuna wedged in a narrow space between the stove and a lopsided dishwasher with a sagging door. I fish it out with the broken off trailer from an old wooden snowshoe I found in Unc's closet. I Clorox the trashcan, then return to the closet.

My daughter wants pictures. She's enamored with sepia tones, bamboozled by the fictions she reads on Forefathers.com. There're no family photos here. Excavating floor bound debris, I unearth an old algebra text, its cover cold to the touch. Dad said his number crunching, bookkeeping father railed when Unc couldn't solve equations. Funny that Unc, no keeper of books, kept this one. A stained exam falls out, Unc's name written in his loopy hand just below the F. A plethora of red ink covers the page. Unc left blank the space demanding the definition of entropy (or one could substitute a formula). The teacher wrote in: The gradual decline of a system, the measurement of its randomness. Synonym: decay.

Between the last page and the back cover is a postcard from Dad. Says he's sending Unc the sum needed to fund the secondhand lunch truck (not a roach coach he hopes, ha-ha) but would Unc please consider a move, join us in Vero Beach? Dad promises to help with a job, an apartment and AA. The flipside of the card shows a tropical sunrise of the ilk I had come to expect as my birthright; Apollo rising for his opening act in a sky marked with the same energetic red wielded by Unc's exasperated instructor. In the limited margin left to him below the photo, Dad signed off with Carpe Diem.

Grateful to have found a memento for my daughter, I put the postcard in my carry-on. On second thought, I add Unc's paper with all its errors. Maybe my daughter can solve for X, when the knowns are a long-lost invite to paradise and a long-ago flunked algebra test.

Post to an Old Lover

For a man so tall, you moved with the grace
of a Trumpeter swan.
I remember the arch
of your back above me,
your neck, undulating.
Come away with me, you said,
long before that was a line
in a vow and promise song.
But I had a mother growing fonder
of the bottle, a thesis to defend,
money owed to an uncle
who signed for my used car.

Come away with me, you said.
You're not the sort of girl to marry
a lawyer, a dentist, a candlestick maker.
But I was.

Friends who followed you on Facebook
reported that you lived your life exactly
as you said you would.
You fished halibut in Norway,
crewed a catamaran to Galapagos,
guided hikers in Tivoli,
cleaned museum artifacts in Mykonos.
Last week, you left a brown-skinned poetess
your widow in a house you hand-built
on a hill in Ecuador.

Friends offered to send me your photo,
the one you posted
days before you died. I said no.
I want to see you as that swan,
take full measure of your wingspan,
strongest of birds, magnificent.
I want to imagine
that I said *yes*, pretend it was me
who coasted, aloft, while you gained the lift,
pumping muscles, cartilage and tendons
to buoy us from below.

What if *I* had believed
you could bear us away,
trusted you not to mire us
in the quicksand that lies
between coming and going.

Friends offered to send me the obituary
your wife wrote. Two pages published
in Portoviejo. Nobody gets that in the US of A.
I said no,
though I'd like to hear it read aloud,
savor the melodious, fluid sounds,
the contours and crescendos,
but I wouldn't grasp the meaning
of the words, written, as they would be,
in a language I never learned.

Photo by Claire Massey

In the Backyard of Childhood

THE LEAVES OF THE MIMOSA tree envelop and conceal me, yet offer spaces between their lacy fingers. These openings I utilize for spying, for monitoring the comings and goings in the backyard of childhood. Usually, it is only the movements of my father's tired bird dog, Tex, who rouses his arthritic legs to follow the altering clumps of shade. Or, my pet mockingbird, who perches on the rim of the dog food bowl, to which Tex, in his old age, is increasingly indifferent. Sometimes, it is just thunderheads, stacking or drifting apart, studied before I open my book. I love to read while stationed in my favorite deep V of my favorite mimosa tree.

Today, it is my model tall, red haired, way too bubbly and always overdressed Aunt Ruby, adjusting her sleek, A-line skirt as she rounds the corner from the carport to the sliding glass door at the back of our house. I watch her without calling out. She re-hoists her black, patent leather purse, de rigueur for 1950s ladies, after she inserts her gloves and snaps shut the faux gold latch.

She will soon be inside, on the couch with my mother, sipping scotch and water from the frosted glass she always accepts when it's offered. My mother and Aunt Ruby will twitter and giggle and wink like school girls, their knees touching, the ears of their conversational subjects, or victims, as my father terms them, burning bright as my aunt's hair. My mother's mood will lift and lighten after this visit, and I make a plan to show her my less than stellar report card as soon as my aunt departs.

Whatever the reason, perhaps in response to some pre-adolescent, moody need for privacy, I stay put in my beloved mimosa this particular afternoon. I stay silent, smug in the knowledge that I'm so well hidden, my aunt can't spot me. Not that I don't adore her, but I don't want to go inside, wash my hands, comb my hair, listen to the two of them speculate as to when I might need a smelly new perm or a training bra. I will skip Aunt Ruby today. She will, after all, be back.

I listen to my aunt's high heels click on the concrete steps and pause at the door, while it whooshes open in its frame and I hear my mother's voice rise in greeting, in welcome.

I cannot know that this small and innocent choice will be my first taste of bitter, adult-like regret.

I cannot know that my Aunt Ruby will soon and suddenly die, felled young by a heart attack that nobody saw coming. She was relaxing on her couch with her husband after dinner, legs tucked primly under her dress, in the way of 1950s ladies. Her red head slumped slowly towards her shoulder. He thought she had fallen asleep.

I cannot know that this will prove to be the first

in a series of blows to my mother, that will dilute her laughter to a faint, fleeting sound, whittle her faith, and render her good health a memory.

I cannot know, that many years hence, when I live far from the backyard of childhood, my father's tree trimmer will have to cut down my mimosa, damaged as it was, in a storm. He will show me there, in the deep V of the uppermost section of trunk, the place where I had taken a pocket knife and carved, in the block letters of a child, "God love us." Funny, I don't remember doing that at all.

Violation

He bargained hard for her blossoms,
then neglected to water or commit to the soil
in the season of nurture that he,
self-important, busy,
ignored.

Finally he notices
ex-flowers in a corner, brittle, dark as smoke,
full heads that nodded, entreated him to plant,
promised to return
splendor,
contracted in rigor mortis.

He thinks of her at work,
touching stems, sating thirst,
fingers plump, tender,
hovering above
drops beading.

He dumps crumpled husks in the trash,
balls the note he found when she left.

What he won't forget was
hope,
the way she tempered her voice to urge
that he angle blinds, balance shadow with sun,
the way budded leaves,
accustomed to protection,
unfurled
and earnest blooms
opened.

Beach Photo

I don't remember
this portable playpen
from the 1950s
with fat, wooden slats
barely permitting
a view of the breakers.

Must have been my third
or second summer?
I look to be
a handful,
mid-century girl-child
howling for freedom,
a bar-rattling,
foot-stomping
rebel.

My mother watches
intently, looks to be
off-kilter,
losing equilibrium,
feet seeking leverage,
in the lopsided sand.

On a boardwalk distant,
my father levels a tripod,
narrows his focus,
closes an eye,
captures his subjects.

Anniversary Presents

LORRAINE CAN JUST REACH Gus's suitcase hibernating in the top closet shelf for God knows how many years. After wrestling it down, she's sure it will never see another spring. Naugahyde chipping, one side bowing in, metal ID plate so worn Gus's initials have nearly disappeared. She decides it will do as a box for the crystal.

Though she has no plans to move, Lorraine has taken to packing odd possessions, canoe paddles and pressure cookers, a telescope, framed photos of bass caught a long time ago. She knows some, like the canoe with its paddles, were anniversary gifts, Gus's celebration of their fifth or their sixth, whatever was the Year of Wood. She packs in the wee hours, past the time her daughter might call, ask whatcha doing, offer nonsense advice that starts with a phrase like, *When Dad gets home…*

Gus got a kick out of following the traditional list of wedding anniversary offerings. Lorraine preferred trips but The List made him happy. She indulged his one and only annual extravagance.

Their fortieth anniversary is Friday. The floor nurse at Trinity Gardens says they can't visit in person but she can stand at the plate glass window. The nurse assured her Gus is not sick. *Except for*, Lorraine thinks, *the MS that gums nerves, jams messages to muscles.*

Lorraine finds the gift card with the aperitif crystal. She had forgotten the name of the pattern. *Embrace.* She reads the company's description, "artfully braided tendrils entwine stems comfortable to hold," beneath which, Gus had simply written, Happy 15th!

Her fifteenth year of marriage. It passed like any other. Quiet. Steady. Perhaps it was the year she discovered gratitude for Gus's difference from her first love or her third. Maybe it was the milestone season for realizing that lust or passion, whatever the name of youth's hunger, was longing that must remain unrequited.

For several years after the crystal anniversary, Gus retrieved the cordials for Thanksgivings, birthdays. He would shush everyone, play the goblets with his fingers, clarion notes pinging at congenial frequencies. Before she washes them, Lorraine flicks her nails on the rim of each already clean, unclouded goblet. She makes them sing. Later, she dries them, turns them in her hand, marvels at their luminosity. Finally, she rolls them in plastic until she can't see through the packets, banishes them to the velvet darkness of Crown Royal bags.

Early Friday morning, she googles The List, laughs when she sees that the fortieth anniversary gift is rubies. Anyone past fifty could tell Hallmark they're all wrong, the years' souvenirs should be reversed.

Emeralds and coral, rubies and pearls mark the spark and promise of early years. It's the practical stuff that memorializes endings–paper, cotton, aluminum, leather. The stuff of prescription pads, nurses' notes, urinals, backless gowns, comfy bedside chairs, cool to the touch.

Lorraine rummages in the dresser, finds her ring with the garnet that looks like a ruby. Gus could celebrate by wearing it on his pinky. Then she remembers. No jewelry permitted at Trinity Gardens.

After lunch, Lorraine drives to the center, squeezes between two bland, close-cropped bushes. She presses the drug store greeting card hard against the glass. Someone wheels Gus closer but he can't decipher small print. She shouts the sappy lines and he smiles. She doubts he heard.

The glass is institutional double pane, smudged with handprints, fogged with breath and the trapped inside air that condenses, smears views. They speak almost in unison. Love you, honey. Happy Anniversary. But this glass is dense, its composition nothing like that of crystal. Never purposed for reunions, it mutes their voices, distorts their faces, blocks every attempt at embrace.

Post-Covid Paradise

Though I did admire the artistry
of costumed humanity,
the sunny arc of beads
defying gravity,

the raucous throng of carnival,
the collective roar of Mardi Gras
was not my Shangri-la.

My idea of paradise
was an umbrella drink
on an empty beach,
a day alone writing

to my heart's content,
a solo voyage on a Sunfish,
distance diminishing
shouts from the shore.

Now, heaven would be a parade,
friends hugging,
strangers' shoulders touching,
hands joining 'round the same shiny throw,
then the swiftly spreading
open-throated, open-handed
letting go.

If I Try Sometime

WAITING FOR THE HUMMINGBIRD, I get the dove. Common, ground dove they call her. She bobs in no hurry, looks over her shoulder for jays and mockers and the Munson's cat that lurks. Finally satisfied for her safety, she accepts, like manna from heaven, the stale, discount seed that others fling from the platform feeder.

Above her head, my deluxe hummer station, real glass double cylinders with painted-on flowers, glints rose and orange and fool's gold yellow in the sun. Top of the line, the clerk assured me, guaranteed to attract the hummer. Forty-nine bucks, even with the coupon from Outside Pleasures.

I keep watch all morning, work on the porch, but nothing much gets done. I write in awkward, jumpy fits and spurts, my gaze diverted from the blinking cursor to my showy circus of a feeder. Impatience blossoms, masses like the passion vine that's swamping the deck.

Where is this bejeweled wonder, with his blur of wings beating at unfathomable speed and his red diamond throat that so bewitches me? What a thrill if he would grant me my moment to bask in his aura of avian royalty. I could brag to my neighbor, the garden club secretary, who claims he breakfasts each morning in *her* yard.

All afternoon and into the evening, I pace back and forth from my desk to the window, drawn like a moth to the beacon feeder. But he's not. There's only the dove.

Dusk comes. I give up on the hummer. That's when I register the sounds I've missed. The dove coos with notes that are symmetrical, predictable. Her rhythmic repetition of a single, low vowel soothes. She doesn't lift, fly up in a glorious burst with a helicopter's whoosh. She hugs the earth. She's drab, it's true, spotted gray and brown, and she shies away from confrontation with other birds. Her life is ordinary, non-migratory. But something about watching her pursue her good luck, her accidental meal of thrown away food, calms the whirr in my head, slows my staccato pulse. Not a sliver of grain, not a strand of husk goes to waste. She is content with the whims of fate.

Hearing the measured beat of coos reminds me the harbingers of peace are doves. While pugnacious hummers can be loud-mouthed warmongers.

An old Rock anthem comes to mind, when I turn on the lamp and close the blinds. Bird watching, after all, is a game of chance. I can sweeten the odds with fresh nectar, watermelon in squirrel proof containers. But you don't always get what you want. I can tell my-self the bird I pursue is rare, capricious, fickle. I can try again tomorrow. Or I can remember what I've for-gotten, to trust in the fruits of the watching. And there just may be, grace enough, for me to get what I need.

PHOTO BY BART DAUGHETY

Choose Florida

Brochures assure
sun gilded retirement, afterglow after
the nest egg cracks open,
cloistered landing in walled reserves
named for vanquished birds,
Falcon's Rest, Osprey Haven.

Architects of artifice render
night artificial in Florida.
Excesses of light double down
on full moons.
Exhausted natives
sing twenty-four hours
while dazzled migrants
lose their way.

Ad execs promise to banish darkness
and eerie, unsettling calls
from screech owls and clapper rails.

Retirees who die after dusk have options
unavailable in scrub brush or marshes.
Byways to life after are lit, asphalted
and though not explicitly stated,
eulogies are provided
by mockingbirds.

Man in the Rainbow River

A Fable for Our Time

WHEN THE RAINBOW RIVER began to speak, the remnant band of creatures eking out a living along its banks was dumbstruck. Divine Dominion being no competition for Manifest Destiny, the ranks of hangers-on were thinning by then but the lone remaining panther, who was barely out of adolescence and a bit full of himself, summoned the hutzpah to organize a community forum. What is needed, he told the leader of the yellow-eared turtles, is an investigative committee. The old guy withdrew to his shell and considered, finally agreeing to send a representative. With the reptiles on board, the panther managed to assemble some shell-shocked deer and twitchy racoons, a patchy feathered marsh hen among assorted wading birds and the silver mullet king, who had suspicious spots on his fins and was not long for this world. Mama vixen promised to attend a meeting if she could bring her kits, humans having ruined her burrow by inserting mothballs and a blaring radio.

Initial discussion pegged the bellow of the fourteen-foot alligator as the culprit but no one had seen him for years. The great egret opined that the gator became dangerously addicted to sunbathing on a goopy mat of algae so substantial it supported his weight. "Thus making him," said the egret, her aquiline beak in the air, "an easy target for those wishing to clear the way for squeamish tubers, drainage pipe layers and private dock erectors." The red striped bass and the indigo snake, their glistening hues fading of late, insisted that the voice in the river had its genesis in man-made conspiracy. The rumbling vibration was the phosphate mine, the aquifer pump, the wave of base noise churned from speakers installed in gazebos that lined the shore. The racket seeped through skin, sabotaged the rhythm of blood exchanging.

Someone nominated the manatee to confront the voice but he was voted down—his kind were lumbering and slow and too dim-witted to avoid their fate. His wife had been killed by a boat with three Evinrude engines and still, he asked where she was. In the end, the task of conversing with the Unknown fell to the panther, who had the stealth and the speed and the smarts, it was generally agreed, to avoid human trickery.

At 3:00 A.M. on a void-of-course moon, the panther crept past lawns reeking of fertilizer. He combat-crawled beyond edgewaters clotting with knotweed. He waded in as far as he dared, which was far for a brash young male. He stopped when the roiling waters of the headspring began to pummel his legs like a riptide. "Who is here?" he called to the churning eddy. "What say you?" he demanded of the swirling vortex. There passed an eternal moment while the panther fought for his footing in fickle, shifting sands. Finally, there arose a grumble, a watery static that began to clear like fog at dawn. The panther deciphered words, then sentences and whole passages, propelled to the surface on the mighty exhalations of the river's deepest boils.

"At last," boomed the baritone voice with imperious tone, "a cognizant audience. You are a sentient being, are you not? And where are the rest of the minions who depend on *moi* for their living?"

The panther had an impulse to crow that he alone had the courage for this chore but with a nod to maturing judgement, he squashed it. "I will interpret your message," he told the voice, adding that it was cold, standing in the river's voracious suck.

"Ah yes, my flow is strong and virile. However, I have noticed there are days when I feel a mysterious pull, an odd tug, as if a drain were—"

"What do you wish to tell us?" interrupted the panther. His claws were numb and losing their grip.

"My life has been the stuff of legends, you know. Did you hear from your great-grandfather or some long lost auntie, how my name was bestowed? My waters were so gin-clear, reflected rainbows arched in my depths, my aqualungs so robust, sapphire streams gushed from my vents. I was liquid light, a fathomless prism, a kaleidoscope of color, a sunken sun mirroring the rise, the dénouement of days."

The panther retreated to a midstream islet once

rooted in the native bullrush that had sheltered otters at play. "Do you wish me to tell of your fading beauty?"

"Why you whippersnapper! Open your eyes! Do you need sunglasses? If you do, there are plenty embedded in my bottom. No problem to flush a pair loose." The voice surged with smug self-assurance. "I want all to know I am lovelier than in days of yore. I host a procession of technicolors that grows grander every summer!"

Though disconcerted to discover the river fancied himself a backdrop for flamboyant flotsam, the panther used his talent for treading softly. "Tell me please," he said, "what evidence do you have for this renaissance? I want to understand, but I am not as wise, as experienced as you."

"Indeed," said the river, mollified. "If you weren't so afraid to be spotted in daylight, you would see I've been upgraded, decorated, twenty-first century style. I'm blessed with a planet-sized palette of hues, a plethora of neon radiance. Have you noticed the cans that bob in the wake of jet skis? Logos of royal blue and blood red, on a background of full moon platinum, dance in Yamaha orchestrated waves. Lime-green floats and plastic dinghies figure-headed with fuchsia-haired mermaids and leaping pink dolphins ply my waters by day. Paddleboards with strip lights the color of sirens pulse after dark, like the fireflies of yesteryear." The river droned on in the flowery language of pride. He was, he told the panther, a veritable parade of wonder, a conduit for discarded beauty. Swirling in foam at his surface, were flashy bags with scarlet targets, striped swim goggles snagged in polka dot panties, bottle shards gleaming gold in effluent. Best of all were oil slicks that slithered through waters where basking turtles once fed. "No one can deny," huffed the river, "petrol reflects every color of the rainbow!"

On the dark of the moon, which wasn't dark due to halogen lights from a golf course that fogged the sky fluorescent-purple, the panther gathered his ragtag crew. They met in a small wooded glen that survived the backhoe. The panther reported the Unknown to be a simple-minded fool, the blustering voice of man-in-the-river, a deluded being blowharding foolishness. There were sighs of relief all around. The yellow-eared turtle said such silly speech sounded harmless enough; the voice should be ignored. A rabbit who wandered in from the ninth hole said the whole affair was sad. It sounded as if the river was suffering some form of aquatic Alzheimer's. Catching sight of the hungry-eyed fox and her scrawny babies, the rabbit sidled away towards a sand trap. No worries, called mama fox, I wouldn't eat you if you were the last hare on earth. I've seen you munch fairway grass! A mild commotion ensued, annoying the blasé egret who moved to adjourn. A battle fatigued racoon, who'd witnessed his daughter treed by dogs, thanked the panther. Then everyone faded into mist, which smelled faintly of Mickey D's and mosquito truck.

In the seasons to come, most gave the voice in the river, rumored to be bat-guano crazy, a wide berth. On occasional forays down the springhead path, the panther hailed him with hello, how you doing, never lingering for serpentine answers. One night, the river asked if he would stop and talk. "I will," said the panther, "but speak up. I'm not wading in your chilly water."

The river gurgled a chuckle. "Oh, I'm not the temperature I used to be." The nuclear plant's tepid discharge crossed the panther's mind but he knew the voice was too irrational to discuss the matter. "I wonder," said the river, "if you've seen any beavers of late, or that oafish manatee. I need someone to trim the emerald green stems that sometimes...seem to stick in my throat, make me...a little short of breath. Just the merest cut, you understand. Have you noticed the lush, leafy arms that undulate in my currents? Why, some of my pools are becoming verdant gardens!"

"Old friend," said the panther, "what you think luxuriant is dangerous. That fecund stuff is hydrilla. It spawns nothing but trouble."

"But it flowers so beautifully! Unlike the dull eelgrass mullets adore. I was happy to host a newcomer. I've been nourishing eelgrass for ages."

"You won't be alive to feed the minions, if that

overgrowth takes you over."

Man-in-the-river whined in a petulant tone, like a child on the brink of a tantrum. "Oh, what would **you** know? It's your kind that's doomed. Everyone knows Florida cougars can't find healthy mates. No doubt your line is inbred."

"If you're going to insult me—" began the panther, but he stopped. The voice lacked resonance, vigor. He heard a reedy quaver that told him the rabbit was right to pity the river. He turned on soundless, padded heels and disappeared.

Years passed. The river waned narrower, weedier, fainter in timbre. Visitors sought footing on buckled, rootless banks. They frowned and shook their heads.

Choking on pondweed and silt, lungs slimed with water hyacinth, the voice could not muster volume to cry **help**. He muttered, whimpered, and mumbled but humans were deaf to mother tongues. There came months of drought so relentless, the river knew he was gasping his last. "What I want," he whispered to the cold, staring stars, the indifferent clouds scuttling past, "is a monument to mark my passing. If I must die a mudhole, too shallow to float flotillas, I want a billboard erected on the spot where my headwaters erupted. I want my name in LED lights every color of the rainbow!" The river prayed to an apathetic sun, pleaded with the heedless wind. No one relayed his final wishes.

The last generation of yellow-eared turtles, alarmed

by increasing salinity, were grateful to be captured, glad to be inmates of the Tampa Zoo. The racoon relocated to the 'burbs. Leftovers left on stoops for cats who supped on songbirds made him jolly and morbidly obese. The egret, with her bill above it all, claimed climate change was a hoax. She flew into a hurricane and was lost. Gator junior, son of the fourteen-footer, heir to king-sized beds of scum, died early from a monofilament mass. The panther, remembered as a talented translator, was killed long ago, hit by a jeepload of texting teens when he crossed Highway 20, looking for love.

Toxic Drift

"Mimosa" means sentient beings,
wild trees with consciousness emitting
from sensitive leaves. Exiled from ordained
Edens, these outcasts took root in my yard.

Bees that were vanquished for years,
like Israelites in the dessert,
return to this untilled half-acre,
anoint in blossoms exhaling
scent of the promised land.

But there are no borders for breezes
bearing a neighbor's poison.

Leaves fold in warning
of treacherous homecoming.
Choreographed steps that tell seekers
the covenant manifests in my backyard oasis
break sequence. The faithful succumb
to fatal dysrhythmia.

The dance of life ceases.
Exodus perennial.

Picnic at Bird Isle

Lurking in sawgrass,
leeward side of the islet,
we spy shells of shotguns,
relics of violence,
of powerful need to wield
insensate power,
deny willets and skimmers
safe harbor.

We spread our picnic
on a blanket distant
from these plastic mementos,
still, neon orange cylinders
lure the sun.

Words boom
in birdless quiet,
then die on our tongues.

We trade deli sandwiches,
pass honeyed wafers
but food has lost
its celebratory flavor.

Towards evening a pontoon listing
with men arrives. They hustle
big-chested coolers
through saltwort and bindweed,
booze in cordgrass
on the windward side.

When they leave, we discover
the goose nest we saw earlier
now harbors smashed eggs
and crumpled, bright cans.

Weighted by the silence
of emptied sky,
we weigh anchor,
forsake keepsakes of Bird Isle,
leave sullied souvenir feathers
of ibis and loon where they lie.

Photo by Bart Daughety

Clean Sweep

TWO HUNDRED MILES from home in a lodge built of cypress, I watch the hurricane bloom on the news. When hawkers of hormones and call anytime lawyers interrupt, I take solace from the window's alternate view. Passion flower and farewell summer, indigenous dwellers on upland savannah, nod heads in a breeze benign and far removed from landfall.

The morning after, a neighbor assures me our inland homes were spared the worse. Storm shutters askew, bashed gutters, yards littered with limbs and mud. *That barrier island*, she says, *saved our butts*.

Driving convoluted detours skirting the coast, I worry. How much longer can an overbuilt sandspit shield mainlanders? Imported palms, the darlings of upscale realtors, have usurped earth hugging yaupon and myrtle. Dunes anchored by saltbush and sea oats once hunkered down shore like sentinels on guard duty. But they've been trampled by tourists, toppled by front loaders, trucked off by city fathers hell bent on parking garages. Live oaks that tame gales when granted life in groves, were winnowed, culled. Discount landscapers scattered scrawny foreign maples on the mall's concrete islands. Neither was up to the job. Eleventh graders slammed councilmen with protest poetry. The mayor no-showed at the eleventh hour. Monarchs, racerunners, beach mice, all evicted. No mercy.

Turning right where the shore road goes left, I am met with the spoils of a wrong-headed war. Nothing here the victor would want. Cell antennas dangle from crumpled towers like weather vanes gone AWOL. Staves of plasticized wood from Keep Out fences pin a golf cart overturned. Pigeons who stole the niches of gulls peck the wiry guts of a neon sign that usually flashes Turn Around, No Access, Private. Snapped cables mass on the beach like malevolent wrack hurled from the sea. Zip line constructors who broke the spine of hummocks fled.

Four nights after homecoming, I sit on my porch, vowing to let mimosa and wild magnolia overgrow the creek border. The finch feeding swamp privet will not be felled. For the sake of unborn salamanders, leaf litter will remain. Still, I worry. What of the fawn who forged at the edge of my woods? Were hummers depending on feeders I had to remove?

The fox who was a kit in May steps from his mangled cover, rotates paddle shaped ears my way. Partners in mental telepathy, we have a history. Still as the eye of a cyclone, he hears what I have to say. *How on earth did you make it? The flooding den, collapsing burrow, the killing wind no small earthbound creature could venture into?*

He fixes his gaze on my face, a seer summoned to a backyard oracle.

Never mind about that. We have our own version of divine providence. Did you notice that the arrogant hawk, who thought himself apex predator soaring over conquered territory, no longer hunts from aloft? Have you heard the bleat of a scurrying rat, caught a glint off fur of a rabbit? I believe that hawk has been swept away, and now, it's time for my supper.

Haiku Day at the Museum of Natural History

Archive I

Dead beetle illumes
Dark space, once iridescent
Star of Madam's brooch.

Archive II

Stuffed Great Owl glaring
Age-old interrogation
Who're you to quell me?

Archive III

Dancing Manta Ray
Leaping clear of ancient waves
Eulogized in shale.

Archive IV

A panther's passing
Recounted on native stone
Instead of asphalt.

I was
the Ivory Billed Woodpecker.

Those who look
for the lost,
the Audubon chapter
of Jefferson parish,
the biology department
of St. Tammany college,
the Cajun in his pirogue
who would keep his own counsel
if he found me,
wander the swamp seeking hope.

When my red-headed, pileated, disappearing
relative appears, the disciples of science
share a modicum of comfort,
shatter the quiet
with educated chatter
that echoes hollow
in the small, secret forest
of empty nest holes.

Only the Cajun paddles further,
reaches the stilled, fallen garden
of sweetgum and sunken
bald cypress, where believers anchor
blackwater boats, keep silent,
prayerful vigil for my ghost.

Stages That Culminate in Grief:

1. Threatened
2. Vulnerable
3. Endangered
4. Extinct

THE IVORY-BILLED WOODPECKER may be the most mourned casualty of our malignant dominion over Mother Nature. This iconic bird and those with the foresight to champion the right of wildlife to live as the creator intended lost every battle of the war with abusive loggers, swamp drainers, scheming developers, dark money politicians and greedy corporations.

Why did we collectively step aside and allow slash-and-burn forces to forever alter the beauty and needful balance of our world? Was it ignorance, indifference, powerlessness?

Repeated expeditions to remote Florida wetlands have failed to produce a single photo of this holy grail. Yet all over the southeast, there is a swelling cult of followers, of dogged pursuers of the dream—to capture a sighting of the ivory-billed.

Surely the passion and persistence of these questers bears testimony to the enormity of our loss, the depth of our grief.

Are we stuck in the stage of Denial?

Shall we transition to Acceptance, the test at the end of the next chapter, the hard work of restitution ahead?

Earth Day 2020

I roam woods nearly empty,
detour to grow distance
when human voices intrude,
entertain a childish notion
that Mother Nature has decided
I should not walk alone.

Is she a hobbled crone,
struggling to follow,
scarred by her rages,
weary from warring
for boundaries, balance?
No, not today. She's agile, young,
as she moves beside me,
keen hearing fine-tuned,
scanning only for subtle,
primal music. If she winces, head covered
against our wailings,
who could blame her?

At trail's end she pauses
with hand upraised, urges
Listen.
No jet engines whining,
no Ditch Witches digging,
no ocean liners churning
waves of white noise.

For the first time, in a long time,
she cocks a pearled,
oyster shaped ear, smiles
like Mona Lisa.

Her firstborns are singing,
the whale, the sandhill crane,
the south wind surging, ebbing,
the undammed river,
murmuring.

PHOTO BY CLAIRE MASSEY

Photo by Claire Massey

Driver Side Window

A poem for my estranged sisters

Penned in the surly, cantankerous Chevy
where the backseat of childhood was beltless,
fogged windows stuck
in half-mast position,
we shoved and kicked, spat
the same fighting words our parents did,
took it out on each other, tangled
flailing limbs in the failed intentions
of beach towels touting Disney princesses
and blankets meant for mythical picnics.

How good it felt to gift myself at age nineteen
with a Toyota I could trust and then, a Subaru,
for turning twenty-seven and a big-hearted,
even-tempered
Volvo, upon the banner year of forty.
From the vantage point of reinforced
windshield,
the shatterproof driver side window,
I travel vistas I choose.

Lost sisters: Let me recommend
a reliable vehicle. Seating is roomy, steering
responsive,
GPS built-in, safety glass dense yet clear.
It defrosts at the push of a button.

Coronasphere

The Adirondack chair envelops me,
realigns me at the center
of my backyard coronasphere.
No electron micrograph, false colored
sticky-ball image
of virus here, where coronas emit
holy rays. And hues are real,
though the spectrum narrows,
squeezed by the limits of human perception,
saturated, mainly,
by human imagination.

Fog droplets cling to catawba trees.
Haloed with auras of resurrection green,
they breathe with respirations,
deep, slow.

The neighbor's daughter bands her forehead
with a garland of clover.
A month ago, she showed off new molars,
crowns of celestial white erupting
from rosy craters. Now she's banned
from coming over.

Petals of sunflowers shoulder together,
seeded nuclei circled, sheltered,
till the cold spell passes.

The trickster evening star appears.
It doesn't look like what it is,
gaseous particles masquerading
as collective body.

Yet I have seen, in wooded night,
St. Elmo's fire and aurora borealis.
I have seen the solar eclipse,
looking, for all the world,
like an opened eye,
fathomless pupil enclosed
by lavender ellipsoid iris.

False colors I suppose.

I don't know the properties of light,
but I know the red wink
of my porch-bound neighbor's corona cigar
signals calm. I know blush-colored rings
around a bowl-shaped moon
mean a luminary holding water,
signaling promise
of cleansing rain.

Those Little Words That Place You

locate you at
the junctions, the wheres where you decide
the rubble goes, deceptively unsubstantial,
small in
stature words you're told
must not be left to
dangle.

Prepositions are propositions for junk disposal,
nearby or underneath or close between.
Out in front obscures the view ahead.
Opt to skirt around, back away, hurtle over?
Either way, you're propelled towards,
taken for
a ride, a fool or all you've got in
reserve.

Prepositions get a bad rap in
poems.
But you could do worse than to end with
words that move you distant from,
above, astride, on top of.
Choose one to pull you through
before you're finish line tired and beyond
is too far to go.

Right Brain Relief

There will be much
you cannot say.

Sculpt pottery or draw,
weave, whittle wood, ink scrimshaw.

There will be pain
of the toxic, contagious kind
that once articulated,
creates mass, solidifies, bars your way,
an iceberg on the dark Atlantic, a Berlin wall,
a monument to rubble after war.

Let words you cannot speak dissolve
on a palette of burnt sienna,
amber-yellow.

Paint a river the color of honey
and sink them in the tannic water
or place them in the shining lips of fish
to be swallowed.

Leave them sealed
in effigies of stone

or evaporating under
a pitiless sun.

Lose them in the mixed media
of a jungle collage.

If they reincarnate,
as whispers in a dream,
unintelligible exhalations
below the threshold
of understanding,
they will be too faint
to haunt,
vapors,
to be absorbed
by a hand-thrown pot,
the heart-shaped amulet
you wear at your throat,
the carved bone that sings,
when you wake and breathe life into art.

PHOTO BY LUKE WALLIN

Old School Dream

Covid 19 rages like a fifties era
tyrannical stepfather who buzz cuts his hair,
embraces wrath of God doctrine,
grounds you for the slightest infraction,
juke joint dancing, wine on your breath,
a seconds late curfew violation.

Last night I dreamed I was retro living
in the Age of Aquarius,
the water bearer's constellation brimming,
spilling overhead.

My boyfriend kissed me
In the commons garden.
Mogen David flowed.
Gently stoned friends smiled,
blessing unguarded union,
him in his surplus bell bottoms,
me with my waterfall hair,
so abundant.

Errands of Salvage

DARRELL PULLS THE FIAT SPIDER to the curb of his ex-house, now owned by Amanda, his ex-wife. He climbs out of the cramped seat and laces the fingers of both hands high over his head to stretch his back.

Megan, his fiancée, leaned on him hard to buy the Fiat, even though he told her the reviewers said it was marginally as comfortable as a canoe. He's sorry he gave in to Megan. The car makes him feel every minute his age. He hopes Amanda won't come out of the house and see the maneuvering it takes to wrestle the empty liquor store boxes out of the back. He fits the smaller sizes in bigger Rubbermaid bins, then bumps a train of containers up the front steps and into the foyer. Winded, he leans against the wall where Amanda has hung the wooden inlay Mayan calendar they bought in Mexico for their fifteenth, or was it twentieth, anniversary. The knife-tongued deity in the center stares back at him, menacing as ever. Darrell can't remember what he's supposed to be lord of—solar eclipses? The equinoxes? The cycle of human consciousness?

He could never get a handle on all Amanda's cycles. The celestial turning of wheels was an enigma too trite to solve. Amanda lived in tandem with the seasons, the phases of the moon, the movement of constellations. Always heeding the "signs." Shaggy woolly-worms meant blizzards. Rising birth rates for boys meant war. Venus ascending assured conception. He hadn't done his part, the years they tried for a baby. Amanda would tell him it was one or two or however many days past her ovulation and she just knew they would conceive their child. But the auction for his warehouse inventory would be postponed, or his flight would be canceled, overnighting him again at the Comfort Inn. Every spring, she would mark up the calendar; *fertilize the hydrangea this week, move the wild magnolia in two, make love on the strawberry moon.* She would frown at his astrological chart, tell him to schedule his root canal in March.

Darrell fingers his carotid artery. When the thumping slows, he descends the stairs to his ex-basement. Time to replace that last step. The wobble throws him off-balance and his knee pain flares. Doc says he ought to think about a replacement.

Amanda is standing over her washing machine. She glances at him, then resumes her study of the cycle indicator. Darrell has an impulse to ask her to look at his stars, tell him if he should put off knee surgery. *A time for every purpose under heaven.*

"Hey you," Amanda says. "I've packed your sweaters and jackets. And I found your Alpine windbreaker." She points to a recycled UPS box by the basement door. "Better take those today. You'll need 'em soon."

"Don't know if I can fit all my clothes in the car this trip," Darrell says. He decides he'll offer to repair the basement step on Sunday. He doesn't want Amanda asking her new neighbor to do it. The guy's retired and they seem to be getting chummy.

"I'm washing your shorts and T-shirts right now," Amanda says. "They were stinky dirty. No hurry on coming back to get them. Summer's a long way off."

"Amanda, I really appreciate—"

"No problem. You don't have a washer for your condo yet and I felt energetic when I got off work." She blows away a gray-blond strand of hair that's wandered too close to her mouth. "I often do, these days. The effect of doing something you love, I guess."

A shoo-in for Story Hour, Amanda won her dream job a few months ago, youth librarian at his ex-neighborhood's branch. Darrell wishes he had some energy. He's feeling that seven a.m. meeting with his sales force. "Anyway," Amanda says, "Your stuff is taking up space where I want shelving for my plants. Getting late in the year, they need to come in."

When Darrell first told Amanda he was in love with Megan, and meant to have her, there were no tears, shouted recriminations, ugly scenes. It was almost as if Amanda felt sorry for him. Oh, she talked a lot, at first. Handed him all the old, cliché-ridden arguments. Ticked off the perils and pitfalls of a May-December romance. "She's nineteen years younger than you," Amanda had reminded him. "What will you do when she wants sex and you're down in your back? And starting over again, at your age, payments on that expensive condo! Lord, the furnishings alone…you'll have to keep working." Amanda's shapely fingers would flutter as she talked, then land gently on his arm, a wise parent steering her child from some dark fate. "I always planned for us to travel in retirement," Amanda said, "Greece in late June, swimming the Aegean Sea."

"You were the one who wanted to travel," Darrell told her, but he knew as soon as he said it, that it wasn't true. He had been looking forward to long, languid journeys. He'd known that Amanda would have planned them all, and that they would have departed and returned at just the right times, the planets auspicious in the sky and the tides in perfect sync with the moon.

Yes, Amanda had kept her dignity alright. Her calm, accepting nature had prevailed. Right on up until she signed for the divorce, she talked about how one had to travel the concentric circles, honor the grand design, understand that their place on the wheel was seasonal, mutable. After the decree, she stopped talking. She never mentioned Megan, the affair, his new life, the future. And yet he lived with these twinges—not of guilt but of fear, the feeling of wrongness, as if his love for Megan was a phenomenon set apart, outside, the natural order of things. As if the Mayan god of time was sticking his tongue out at him, dismissing this mortal's revolt as beneath contempt.

The washer dings its finish and Amanda pulls out his cut-offs and short-sleeved tees.

"All your books from the barrister book case upstairs are packed," Amanda says. "There's a dolly up there too, you can take them today."

Darrell remembers with a pang his lovely coffee table editions, the homes of Frank Lloyd Wright, the vintage aircraft of WWII. Megan has made it clear she doesn't want books "cluttering" the condo, she doesn't read much anyway, just five minutes here and there on some website on her phone.

"Would you like to keep them?" Darrell asks.

Amanda watches his face. "If you think that would be best."

Darrell carries boxes of clothes, a few framed prints and some classic wines, (which Meagan did want) to the trunk of his car. He resolves to ignore the throb that is starting behind his kneecap. When he's finished loading, Amanda stands at the threshold of his ex-front door, serene as usual. He wants to say he is grateful for this kindness. That he knows her tolerance for his serial visits is a gift. The afternoon sun halos her pale hair. His own hair is peppering unevenly, not graying well, sprouting patches the color of dirty snow, which Megan's stylist wants to dye.

"I'll hang onto your summer clothes," Amanda calls to him. "It's fall, Darrell. It's getting cold."

Amanda shuts the door. Darrell starts the car. Not ready to pull away, he looks at the big sycamore that was a sprig in his ex-yard when he and Amanda bought the place. The season has slipped up on him, unawares, but now he sees, that it is indeed, fall. The leaves of the sycamore are browning, their edges curling and thinning like old paper. He watches leaves that can't hang on in the stiffening wind let go, drift down with a final twirl and bow, descend with what Amanda would call grace.

Darrell tunes the radio to smooth jazz, a station he doesn't get to hear when Megan is in the car. He's running out of reasons to visit his ex-home. Amanda told him she was going to Workshop Saturdays at the Home Depot, and she could manage the loose step just fine. He takes a long look around the front yard, all the lush vines and bushes that Amanda has planted and tended through the years. The condo complex is cookie cutter, over landscaped, with bland gravel walkways, lattice facades hiding dumpsters, fast-growing, shallow-rooting, non-native pines, planted in unnatural rows.

It's only four, and the sun is out but the air is chilling. Darrell feels, more than sees, dusk coming on. He's never really liked fall. He decides to text Megan, ask her to have a drink with him at The Colonnade, his favorite bar. But hadn't she called the place dated, stuffy? Too bad, he was going to miss the swift, quiet service, the wood burning fireplace and the generous, reliable pours. Maybe they could compromise on the Perimeter Garden Marriott. Megan liked the gaudy, colored lights strung across the verandah, winking on and off like stuck blinkers. He'll savor his Dewars on the rocks and think of the velvety inside of her thighs. He won't notice it getting dark. He won't feel the cold; the place has outside heaters at every table. He won't look at the sweet gums, the oaks and hickories, that surround the courtyard, their leaves falling faster than the staff can blow them away, the tired trees of fall, as Amanda called them. Every year she would tell him that the heartier species, with their deep tap roots, had nothing to fear from the brief, sunless days. *Don't be uneasy, Darrell. The winter solstice is a blessing. The season to mend, to rest, is coming.*

Safe House

Waking in my grandmother's flowing toga
of a nightgown, I fan silken folds
into wings, rise from her bed,
a nymph astride Pegasus, glide
the length of her long, long hallway
to the wide kitchen table offering
fried eggs and homemade fig jam, the secret
sugared coffee she allows me.

I am light in my child body,
I am porous and shining
in the unaccustomed light
of a many windowed home,
winging toward grace, metamorphosis.
My parents' bleak house
is shuttered and sold. Remembering won't slow
my momentum in the long, long run
because this morning I am airborne
in the break-fast-fragrant passage
of my grandparents' home. They are calling
me to come, come on, and I am soaring
in homespun finery, flying
into what will become
soul-saving memory, the halcyon moment
of the lightness of being.

Mark as Read

the poem about your little dog and you
huddled in a closet meant for brooms,
driven by the storm's fury
from your writing room
beside the aging tulip poplar,
vulnerable to lightning
and still trying
to bloom.

Mark as justified

the use of guise,
your fine-tuned master's voice contrived
to slow the rhythm of her trembling,
your lullaby of verse
that seemed to shield you both
from thunder gods.

Mark as understood

the impotence of poets
posturing with words,
blustering through tempests,
whistling past the haunts
of Zeus and Thor.

Still, when your next poem arrives
about fragile fans of pen shells
surviving full moon tides
or the battered poplar flowering
despite the odds,
I'll send it to my archives,

Mark it saved,

worthy as gospel
of sacred space
on my hard drive.

Statistics, Analytics and Anecdotal Evidence

APROPOS OF NOTHING, as I've not been caught breaking them, my husband repeats the rules. "Vetted truths only," he says, "fact checked sources, no heresy from Facebook, no re-twittered nonsense."

Like wrestlers priming for a match, we circle one another on the screened porch before manning battle stations from opposing chairs. It's time for another sunrise round of The Feel Better Game. "When have I ever cheated?" I toss back another expresso, visualize the most promising contenders from the datums, factoids and demographics I downloaded last night. I'm sure my husband fattens his favorites file too, on the bad-news evenings before our morning competitions.

"You had a cheat sheet in the pocket of your nightshirt last week."

"Did not."

"Did too."

I did. No printouts allowed but it's hard to lose when short term memory takes a hiatus. Since Covid deprived the world of three million wise elders, gun violence took first place for child mortality and greed obliterated black rhinos, we've sought consolation in our coffee hour showdowns. The object of which is to one-up each other with *happy* facts till a clear winner emerges—the heavy hitter phenomenon that Most Amazes. Astonishes. Restores Wonder. Now that it's impossible to join John Lennon in imagining there's no country, no dogma to kill or die for, we verbally spar for mutual comfort while the sun drives the dark from our yard.

"You first," he says with magnanimity, legs fully stretched, body language meant to convey exaggerated confidence.

I picture my front runners, begin with, "the bloom of scab on your nephew's knee morphed to meshed, virgin skin in twelve hours."

"Anecdotal."

"Observed phenomena. Firsthand!"

"Okay. Don't get excited. It's a giveyou but I'll count it." If my voice rises, he'll shush me, as if neighbors were half-awake children, listening down the hall.

"Tonight, on our Walmart telescope," he says, "we'll see light from six hundred stars that died eons ago."

"Barely a five on the Wonderment Scale. And a suspiciously rounded number," I add.

"LiveScience's actual count was 611, smarty-pants. Verify at http—"

"Oh, never mind." I listen to a freshening breeze, an anomaly for August, a whispered rehearsal for fall. I conjure my Gallup News screen. "One human male, just one, can potentially produce two thousand offspring." My smile is snooty but instantly he returns the serve.

"That's reassuring? Hasn't Homo sapiens bungled his reign?"

"Maybe," I concede. "Withdrawn."

He leans forward, rubs his hands together, signals a slam dunk is coming. "A study of one hundred hummers revealed these birds smell dangerous chemicals in milliseconds. Formerly thought to have no sense of smell."

Pin oak leaves clatter down the street, as if summoned by wind to chase heat out of town. When I point out the sound, he tells me I stall with irrelevant asides. I go for a double whammy. "Dragonflies identify each other by the mosaic of colors in their compound eyes. Paper wasps keep the peace by committing to memory friend's and foe's faces." He arches an eyebrow. I nod vigorously. "New York Times. Or Scientific American."

He reminds me of his right to check my sources, munches an outsized bite of cinnamon roll, talks with food in his mouth. "If one eye is blinded by chemical injury, acuity in the good eye increases in 48% of cases, sometimes returning to 20/20. Johns Hopkins. Since you're cheating with two in a row, so will I. You'll love this one. Sixty-two percent of physicists believe in a supreme being. One third of the highly educated believe in ghosts."

"Of course, silly. Years after he died, a purveyor of homegrown tomatoes came regularly to my great aunt's door."

"Hearsay."

"Not meant for entry. True story." An inch-long tree frog sticky foots across the porch screen in a synchronized dance of grasp and release. I think of describing the incredible choreography but switch instead to, "Thirteen world governments have finally admitted little green men walk the earth. No harm intended." Chin in the air, I quote astronomers, astronauts, the air force.

He smiles with annoying indulgence, takes another hit of Joe. "I'll bite but that's no winner. Try harder."

"Your father in the memory unit, who no longer eats solid food, remembers verbatim a ditty his mother taught him. Says she fed him words in a dream."

"Anecdotal," he groans, "Again."

I distract him from any thought of reprimand he might be entertaining. "*Listen*." Somewhere in the stirring neighborhood, Stevie Wonder unravels his ribbon in the sky. Keyboard so haunting, so miraculous, I shiver. Finally, my husband cocks his head, hears, absorbs. I prime him for my piece de resistance. "Systematic research can be manipulated. Just because case studies rely on personal observation—"

"Okay, okay. Last chance."

The toe pads of the tree frog flash neon in the risen sun. I wonder what this tiny amphibian makes of our artificial barrier, our impermeable landscape of wire. Surely, he finds it unknowable, undivinable, as the round planet was to medieval flat-earthers. It comes to me then, like a photographic memory. The winner.

"A marine biologist in Alaska keeps a tropical octopus tanked in his home. The octopus watches TV through the glass while holding arms with his favorite human, the scientist's daughter. Entwined like teenagers at the late, late show, they watch undersea documentaries. When his cuttlefish cousins hover on the screen, the octopus squeezes her arm, changes color. Not the mottled purple of aggression or self-protection but the baby pink flush of love."

"Well, well," my husband says. We take our demitasse cups to the kitchen sink.

"Well, what? Do you feel better?"

"As a matter of *fact*, I do. Love transmitted through tentacles? A TV watching cephalopod who blushes like a human? Wow." He glances at the clock, plops in front of his computer, where breaking news threatens to break our tenuous mood. "You have time for a victory lap before work."

"Are you fact checking my showstopper, vetting the octopus story? I've already sent you the link."

"Nope. I'm taking it on faith."

"Faith?" My turn to smirk. "Faith is the hope for what can't be proved."

He spins to face me in the ergonomic chair he researched for weeks before clicking Buy. "And hope springs eternal, doesn't it?" His smile is guileless. Beatific. He swivels back to the screen; loads a film I haven't seen on the range of emotions an octopus signals in technicolor. He *does* feel better.

I hum Stevie Wonder, lace up my runners, open the door to light that traveled ninety-four million miles to reach us in eight minutes. (Last Thursday's winner, my husband's submission.) I hit my stride when I round the corner, pass a neighbor retrieving his morning paper. *Don't open it yet* I want to yell. I just scored a ten on the Wonderment Scale.

Sleepless in Her Studio

Triplet muses wake her.
Lucidity breaks the seal of covers.
Restoration shakes her futon bier.
Liberation smacks lips
swollen with voices against exposed ears,
demands she hear,
translate dreamscape to real,

reshape stiffened brushes till supple,
refill inkwells,
scrape clotted paint from horizons,
recall lines erased in poems redacted,
design roofless space that compels
restless graces to settle, dwell.

Now is the time to take back dawn,
stretch vanishing points to infinity.
Candles are lit, the wine holds its breath.
The past has dried on the walls.

ACKNOWLEDGMENTS

Heartfelt gratitude to Luke Wallin, author, cover designer and writing mentor to me and countless students of the craft fortunate enough to know him.

Sincere appreciation to Diane Skelton, author, editor and publishing consultant, whose patient guidance made this collection possible.

Many thanks to the editors and staff of the following publications in which these works first appeared.

"Island of Lost Boyfriends" ▸ *Bright Flash Literary Review*

"Subtext of a Prayer" ▸ *Writing in a Woman's Voice*

"Spanish Lessons" ▸ *The Emerald Coast Review*

"Last Light at Suwannee River State Park" ▸ *The Pen Woman*

'Tantrum on the Beach" ▸ *Saw Palm Journal of Florida Literature and Art*

"Cigarettes and Scratch-offs" ▸ *POEM*

"In a Wayward Garden" ▸ *Barely South Review*

"A Formula for Entropy" ▸ *Wilderness House Literary Review*

"Post to an Old Lover" ▸ *The Avalon Literary Review*

"Violation" ▸ *Panoply*

"Anniversary Presents" ▸ *The Pen Woman*

"Choose Florida" ▸ *Lucky Jefferson 365 Collection*

"Toxic Drift" ▸ *Tiny Seed*

"Clean Sweep" ▸ *Halfway Down the Stairs*

"Haiku Day at the Museum of Natural History" ▸
Bear Creek Haiku

"Earth Day 2020" ▸ *Flights*

"Driver Side Window" ▸ *The Dead Mule School
of Southern Literature*

"Coronasphere" ▸ *Persimmon Tree*

"Those Little Words That Place You" ▸ *Flashes of Brilliance*

"Old School Dream ▸ *Writing in a Woman's Voice*

"Mark as Read" ▸ *POEM*

"Sleepless in Her Studio" ▸ *Snapdragon:
A Journal of Art and Healing*

ABOUT THE COVER ARTIST: LUKE WALLIN

Luke is a writer and visual artist from Mississippi. Love of the wild fills his books and paintings. He has written eight award winning books for children and young adults, and, with his daughter Eva Sage Gordon, wrote *The Everything Guide to Writing Children's Books, 2nd edition*.

Luke holds an M.F.A. in Fiction Writing from Iowa, as well as advanced degrees in Philosophy and Regional Planning. He wrote *Conservation Writing: Essays at the Crossroads of Nature and Culture*, and co-editied the anthology *Nature and Identity in Cross-Cultural Perspective,* with Irish geographer Anne Buttimer.

Luke taught Philosophy at Manhattan's School of Visual Arts, Literature as a Fulbright Professor at University College Dublin, Creative Writing in Spalding University's M.F.A. in Creative Writing Program, and now is Professor Emeritus of English at The University of Massachusetts Dartmouth.

When he retired from UMass Dartmouth in 2008, Luke wanted to study photography and painting. He had long admired the painting of Mary Elizabeth Gordon, an artist, illustrator, art professor, and his wife. He was also inspired by the painter Dennis Pearson,

a friend since childhood, and by Lloyd Kelly, Jr., a professional artist and friend for decades. Lloyd gave Luke painting lessons, Mary shared her art supplies, and Dennis was generous with suggestions.

Luke's artwork has appeared in the magazines *Sisyphus*, *Canary*, *The Louisville Review*, *Penumbra*, and in private collections. These days he loves painting with gouache, often in his wildflower garden.

Contact Luke at reddogmoon@gmail.com.

ABOUT THE AUTHOR: CLAIRE MASSEY

Claire believes that our need to share the healing energy of creative works has never been greater. It is our stories that save us, whether they be poems that portray the human condition, tales that inspire us to champion nature or memoir that exposes the powerful truths that confront us during routine moments of our everyday lives.

After retiring from a decades-long career as a Speech-Language Pathologist, Claire is grateful for the opportunity to reunite with the muses of creativity and resume the writing life. To date, her poetry and prose have appeared in more than thirty venues and journals of the literary and visual arts.

She is poetry editor for *The Pen Woman*, the quarterly magazine of the National League of American Pen Women, and former poet laureate for the Pensacola, Florida, branch of this organization. Her short stories, flash memoir and poetry have garnered awards from the Pen Women National Biennial Competition, the Pen Women Florida State Association, the National Soul-Making Keats Literary Competion and the West Florida Literary Federation (now Emerald Coast Writers). She was invited to read her fiction on Tennessee Public Radio and to present her memoir at San Francisco, California's main library, as part of the 2017 Soul-Making Keats program.

PHOTO BY ANNE BAEHR

She served as selection editor/prose editor for the 2019 and 2021 print editions of *The Emerald Coast Review*. In 2021, she designed a virtual workshop titled, "Writing with Precision and Power: Exploring Short Forms of Prose."

Claire studied creative writing at The University of Tennessee, The University of Southern Mississippi and through The University of Iowa Guided Correspondence Study. She holds B.S. and M.A. degrees from the University of Tennessee in Knoxville.

A member of the Florida Writers Association, she resides in Navarre, Florida, where she finds joy in supporting literary artists who move us beyond the boundaries of concrete thinking and further our quest for understanding of self and the world.